FOOD MATTERS

PROCESSED FOODS

by Rebecca Rissman

Content Consultant
Alex Kojo Anderson, PhD
Associate Professor of Nutrition
University of Georgia

Core Library

An Imprint of Abdo Publishing
abdopublishing.com

abdopublishing.com

Published by Abdo Publishing, a division of ABDO, PO Box 398166,
Minneapolis, Minnesota 55439. Copyright © 2016 by Abdo Consulting
Group, Inc. International copyrights reserved in all countries. No part of
this book may be reproduced in any form without written permission from
the publisher. Core Library™ is a trademark and logo of Abdo Publishing.

Printed in the United States of America, North Mankato, Minnesota
042015
092015

THIS BOOK CONTAINS
RECYCLED MATERIALS

Cover Photo: Shutterstock Images
Interior Photos: Shutterstock Images, 1, 36; James Ambler/BMUSA/
Getty Images, 4; Richard B. Levine/Newscom, 6, 28; iStockphoto, 8;
Imaginechina/AP Images, 10; Justin Lane/EPA/Newscom, 12; Bettmann/
Corbis, 14; Dominic Lipinski/Press Association/AP Images, 20; Sam Riche/
The Indianapolis Star/AP Images, 22; William Archie/Detroit Free Press/
MCT/Newscom, 25; Michael J. Ermarth/US Food and Drug Administration,
34; Alena Haurylik/Shutterstock Images, 39, 45; Jonathan A. Meyers/Stock
Connection Worldwide/Newscom, 40

Editor: Mirella Miller
Series Designer: Becky Daum

Library of Congress Control Number: 2015931601

Cataloging-in-Publication Data
Rissman, Rebecca.
 Processed foods / Rebecca Rissman.
   p. cm. -- (Food matters)
Includes bibliographical references and index.
ISBN 978-1-62403-867-9
1. Processed foods--Juvenile literature. 2. Processed foods--Health
aspects--Juvenile literature.   I. Title.
664--dc23

                                                    2015931601

CONTENTS

THE PROCESSED FOOD FIGHT

n 2010 photographer Sally Davies started a new art project. She placed a fast-food meal from McDonald's on a plate and took a photo of it. She left the meal out overnight. The next day, she took another photo. She repeated this process for six months. The fast-food burger and fries remained almost unchanged. They did not grow mold or rot, even after months of being in open air.

Sally Davies' "Happy Meal Project" serves as a reminder of the amount of processing fast food can undergo.

Fresh food items, such as romaine and arugula, are minimally processed before being sold in grocery stores.

The food did not even smell. Davies' work became instantly famous. People were shocked. Why was the McDonald's meal not decaying? Scientists and consumers weighed in. They guessed the fast-food meal was heavily processed. McDonald's defended their meal. They reported it was made from healthful, natural ingredients. McDonald's said the meal had no preservatives and was only cooked with salt and pepper. But if that was the case, why did the meal not rot?

What Are Processed Foods?

Foods that are processed are altered to make them easier to consume. They may be frozen or packaged. Processed foods are convenient for people or families with busy lifestyles. Processed foods may also feature added ingredients that enhance their flavor or make them last longer. Heavily processed foods

Grocery stores are full of a variety of packaged cookies and other treats.

include packaged cookies or crackers. These foods usually include many ingredients. Minimally processed foods include packaged spinach or precut carrots. They usually have only a few ingredients.

When heavily processed foods first entered grocery stores in the early 1900s, consumers were thrilled. People thought of them as a wonderful technological advance. Processed cheese slices that could last weeks without rotting was exciting. Cookies that came ready to eat were an easy alternative to baking. Homemakers were freed from making their own pasta, bread, yogurt, and other common foods. This gave them time to do other activities. Processed foods made preparing meals easy. Homemakers did not have to spend all day cooking meals for their families to enjoy.

Yoga Mats and Bread

In early 2014, a blogger wrote that the bread at Subway, a popular sandwich restaurant, included a dangerous chemical. Media reports said the chemical also was found in yoga mats. The chemical additive, called azodicarbonamide, actually appears in approximately 500 other processed food products. The Food and Drug Administration (FDA) has ruled that the chemical additive is safe to eat in small amounts. The additive makes rubbery products, such as yoga mats, soft and flexible. It also creates a light and spongy texture in some foods. Subway

Subway used azodicarbonamide to strengthen and bleach their bread dough.

used azodicarbonamide in safe, approved levels. But it soon removed the ingredient from its bread. The reactions of the media and the public threatened to hurt sales.

The Processed Food Controversy

In the past few decades, processed foods have become controversial. They often contain high amounts of sugar, fats, and salt. These ingredients are harmful when eaten in large amounts. As more people become overweight and obese, some critics blame processed foods. They think the added ingredients in processed foods are unhealthy.

Processed foods often contain additives, such as preservatives and food coloring. Preservatives are chemicals used to make foods last longer without rotting. Food coloring is an edible dye that is often made from artificial chemicals. Some people wonder if eating these additives could harm humans in the long term.

Approximately 70 percent of the average American's calories come from processed foods.

Many Americans eat a large amount of processed foods. Calories are the unit used to measure the energy in the foods we eat. Most Americans get less than half of their calories from whole foods. Whole foods are foods that have not been processed or that have been minimally processed. Apples and carrots are examples of whole foods. Because so much of the American diet is processed, it is important to understand what is in processed foods and how they might affect your health.

FURTHER EVIDENCE

Chapter One explains what processed foods are, and it discusses the controversy that surrounds them. What is one of the main points of this chapter? Which pieces of evidence support this point? Go to the website below and find a fact that supports this chapter's main point.

Eat Right
mycorelibrary.com/processed-foods

THE SURPRISING HISTORY OF PROCESSED FOODS

P rocessed foods might seem like a modern idea. But they are not. Humans have been processing foods for thousands of years. Ancient people used salt, fats, or spices to cure meat. This helped it last longer before rotting. They also used fermentation to cure their foods. Fermentation uses substances such as bacteria to change a food item to make it last a long time. Soy sauce and sauerkraut

Native Americans in the early 1900s salted and smoked their meat to keep it fresh longer.

are examples of fermented foods still eaten today. Early people also used many other ancient methods to process foods. These methods helped foods last longer and taste better. As time marched on, food processing became more sophisticated.

Processed Foods and Wartime Diets

The United States experienced a processed foods boom in the 1900s. Between the start of World War I (1914–1918) and the end of World War II (1939–1945), many new processed foods were created. Soldiers fighting all over the world needed good, unspoiled foods to eat. Food scientists worked quickly to create processed foods for them. Instant coffee and Kraft tinned cheese were processed foods that US soldiers relied on during World War I. Other processed foods later became important parts of a military diet. SPAM is a processed pork product that comes in a convenient can. It was shipped to soldiers all around the world during World War II. The US military bought approximately 150 million pounds (63 million kg) of SPAM during the war.

After World War II, processed foods continued to develop. In 1957 a groundbreaking liquid sugar substitute was created. High-fructose corn syrup was inexpensive to make. And it was easy to dissolve in other foods. Most importantly it had a sweet and delicious taste. Food scientists soon started using it in many different processed foods. High-fructose corn syrup

History of Food Science

The first food science department was founded at the University of Massachusetts Amherst. In 1913 Dr. Walter Chenoweth began experimenting with ways to preserve fruits. Soon a group of scientists were busily working together on this project. Food preservation was especially important during World War I. Many people suffered from food shortages. By 1918 the food science department became an official part of the university. Today there are food science departments at colleges and universities all around the world.

Food	Amount of Added Sugar
6 ounces (170 g) fruit-flavored yogurt	7 teaspons (28 g)
1 muffin	7 teaspoons (28 g)
1 tablespoon (15 g) ketchup	1 teaspoon (4 g)
1 cup (8 oz) pasta sauce	4 teaspoons (16 g)
2 tablespoons (30 g) fat-free salad dressing	2 teaspoons (8 g)

The Surprising Amount of Added Sugar

Sugar is a common additive found in processed foods. The American Heart Association recommends limiting added sugars to six teaspoons for women and nine teaspoons for men per day. One teaspoon of sugar is equal to approximately four grams. Based on this chart, how can you make smarter food choices each day when choosing between favorite processed foods?

replaced sugar in many foods and drinks, including most kinds of soda pop.

The Fast-Food Revolution

Processed foods played a huge part in the rise of fast-food restaurants. In the 1950s and 1960s, fast-food restaurants began to pop up all over the United States. They sold fast, cheap meals. Many of the foods served at these restaurants were processed.

By the 1970s, processed foods had changed the way many people ate. They made cooking fast and easy. They also made eating out inexpensive and quick. People got used to the convenience of processed foods. Fewer families stayed home to cook and eat together. The families who did cook used many processed foods to make the job easier. And because of this, fewer children learned from their parents how to cook unprocessed foods.

YOUR LIFE
Your Pantry

One common reason foods are processed is to make them last longer. Fresh whole foods usually last only a short time. Preservatives and other chemicals added to processed foods help them to stay fresh for long periods of time. Have you ever wondered how long some processed foods can last? Go to your pantry and do some detective work! Look on the packaging of processed foods for the expiration dates. Check cans, boxes, and bags. Are you surprised by some of the dates? Which foods last the longest?

Significant weight gain has become a concern for many people in the United States.

Health Consequences

Processed foods may change people's health. The high levels of fats and sugar in some processed foods can be harmful when eaten in large amounts. People who consume too many of these unhealthy foods can develop health problems. Weight gain, obesity, and diseases, such as diabetes, can all come from an unhealthy diet and lifestyle. Not all processed foods make people unwell. In fact, many processed foods are fortified. This means vitamins and minerals have been added to them. Fortified processed foods can be a good source of healthy nutrients.

In the past 100 years, processed foods have changed dramatically. They went from being novelty items that made life a bit easier for home cooks and soldiers to items that are incredibly common. Many people rely on processed foods. They are firmly rooted in the American diet. How this will affect Americans in the future is difficult to predict. Processed foods may become healthier and more nutritious. Or they may continue to pose a health threat if eaten in excess.

EXPLORE ONLINE

Chapter Two details some of the history of processed foods. One ingredient it mentions is high-fructose corn syrup. As you know, every source is different. The website below also discusses high-fructose corn syrup. How is the information on the website different from the information in this chapter? Which information is the same? What new things did you learn from the website?

Is Sugar So Bad?

mycorelibrary.com/processed-foods

CHAPTER THREE

THE SCIENCE BEHIND PROCESSED FOODS

Processed foods are found in nearly every grocery store and supermarket in the United States. They are so common most people do not even think about them. But what exactly are processed foods? And who creates them?

Many heavily processed foods come from the desks, labs, and brains of food scientists. These science professionals work hard to find new ways

Some food scientists work to create new flavors for foods.

to cook, package, flavor, and preserve foods. Food scientists have many different jobs. One of their most important tasks is to make sure the foods they create are delicious. They tweak and adjust recipes to make foods appealing. They occasionally use additives to improve the taste of foods. Additives can change the flavor, smell, and texture of foods. Common additives are sugar, fats, high-fructose corn syrup, and salt. Some additives are healthy. Vitamins and minerals can be added to foods to make them more nutritious.

Food Science Careers

Food science is a rapidly growing field. It appeals to many types of professionals, from chemists to researchers to chefs. Food scientists often work for food companies, universities, or even the government. Their jobs span a wide range. Some food scientists work in kitchens, experimenting with new recipes. Others work with food packaging. Some food scientists work in laboratories, experimenting with new chemicals that may be added to foods in the future. Other food scientists work to make sure foods are produced safely.

Food scientists use the ratings given by taste testers to improve their products.

Taste Testers

Many people work together to make processed foods taste as good as possible. Food scientists often ask taste testers to sample different foods. These tasters rate the foods on their appearance, flavor, texture, and smell. They even rate the sound the foods make when they bite into them.

Keeping Processed Foods Fresh

In addition to improving the flavor of foods, a common reason for processing is to make foods last longer. One way food scientists do this is by removing the water from foods. This process is called dehydration. Moisture causes foods to spoil faster. Dehydrating foods helps them to last longer. Another way to make foods last is to add preservatives. These chemicals help foods stay fresh.

The science behind processed foods advances each day. Many people are excited by the rapid developments in food processing. But many others are worried. They fear heavily processing foods may contribute to a health crisis. Learning more about each side is a great way to get a more complete picture of the controversy.

This excerpt comes from an article Michael Moss wrote for the *New York Times*. He talks about how food scientists work with taste testers to create the very best flavor in processed foods:

> In the process of product optimization, food engineers alter a litany of variables with the sole intent of finding the most perfect version (or versions) of a product. Ordinary consumers are paid to spend hours sitting in rooms where they touch, feel, sip, smell, swirl and taste whatever product is in question. Their opinions are dumped into a computer, and the data are sifted and sorted through a statistical method called conjoint analysis, which determines what features will be most attractive to consumers. . . .

Source: Michael Moss. "The Extraordinary Science of Addictive Junk Food."
New York Times Magazine. *New York Times Company, February 20, 2013.
Web. Accessed November 8, 2014.*

What's the Big Idea?

Review this passage closely. What is Moss saying about the way processed foods are created? Pick two or three details he uses to support his point. What do you notice about Moss's vocabulary? Does this affect the way you read the passage?

CHAPTER FOUR

FACTS ABOUT PROCESSED FOODS

Processed foods are at the center of a heated debate. Some people believe they are harmful. Others praise them for their ease and convenience. So are processed foods good, bad, or somewhere in between?

There are many benefits to processed foods. One benefit is they have a long shelf life. Processed foods stay fresh in pantries, refrigerators, and freezers

Canned vegetables can last for long periods of time in pantries.

Processed Foods and Soldiers

Processed foods have played a large role in wars throughout history. In the American Civil War (1861–1865), soldiers had simple processed foods, such as biscuits and salted and dried meat. These meals later became more sophisticated and tasty. Now soldiers have Meals, Ready-to-Eat (MREs). These processed meals are high in nutrients and calories. Most MREs include an entrée, such as a pasta dish, and a side dish, such as fruit. They often contain bread, dessert, candy, seasonings, and a powdered beverage. One very popular MRE among US troops includes spaghetti and meatballs.

for long periods of time. An unopened can of soup usually lasts between two and five years. A frozen TV dinner will last between six and eighteen months.

Processed foods are often easy to prepare. This is very helpful for busy families who have little time for cooking. Processed foods are often sold ready to eat. Others require only a few steps and ingredients to prepare. Families can pick up complete meals from fast-food restaurants in just minutes, without preparing anything themselves. For families on the go, processed foods are a very tempting mealtime option.

Another benefit of processed foods is they often have vitamins and minerals added to them. For people who do not have access to these nutrients, processed foods can be very helpful. Many breakfast cereals are fortified with iron, vitamin B12, and vitamin D.

One of the strongest selling points for processed foods is that they can be very inexpensive. Families can buy more food for less money. This has great appeal for families struggling to pay for foods.

Concerns about Processed Foods

Processed foods have many negative features. They are often very unhealthy. Additives such as fats, salt, and sugar enhance the flavor of these foods. But they can be harmful in excess. Processing foods also eliminates some of their natural nutritional value. When grains are processed for breakfast cereals, they can lose healthy fiber, vitamins, and minerals. Health

Item	Time to Prepare	Cost
Frozen pizza	20 minutes	$5
Homemade pizza • Crust • Sauce • Toppings	• 60 minutes • 30 minutes to stew • 10 minutes to clean, chop, and shred	$11 • Flour, oil, salt, and yeast ($1) • Fresh tomatoes, olive oil, fresh basil, salt, and pepper ($5) • Cheese, peppers, onions, and mushrooms ($5)

Cost and Preparation of Processed Meals
This chart compares the preparation time and cost of a heavily processed meal with an unprocessed meal. Which meal is faster to create? Which is less expensive? After reading about the pros and cons of processed foods, would you choose a frozen pizza or a homemade pizza?

scientists worry that the large amount of processed food in modern diets has contributed to the rise in serious health problems, such as obesity and diabetes.

Another common complaint about processed foods is they do not contain the bacteria naturally found in some whole foods. Humans need a balance of bacteria in their digestive systems to stay healthy. If they do not get enough bacteria from their food, they can develop health problems, such as weight gain.

The long ingredients lists found on many processed foods are a source of worry for some consumers. Preservatives, food coloring, and artificial flavors are found in many processed foods. The FDA approves these additives as safe. However some people are skeptical about them. They worry these additives could have negative health effects on people in the future.

Everyone must weigh the pros and cons of processed foods for him

YOUR LIFE
How Long Will Your Cookies Last?

Try this experiment to see how preservatives affect your foods. Place one homemade cookie and one processed cookie on a clean plate. Leave the plate in a dry area where it will not be touched by people or animals. Then watch what happens. Every day record in a journal how each cookie changes. Pay attention to the size, color, and smell. After one month, review your results, and then throw out both cookies!

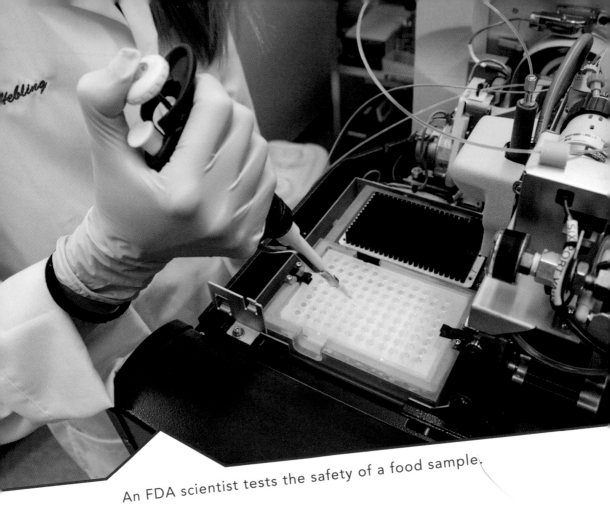

An FDA scientist tests the safety of a food sample.

or herself. The benefits of taste, convenience, and price must be considered alongside the potential health consequences.

This quote comes from Melanie Warner's book, *Pandora's Lunchbox*. Warner discusses the struggle food companies have balancing natural, whole ingredients and processed ingredients in their foods:

> *You might think that having a product contain actual tomatoes or real blueberries would be a good thing. But when processed food is concerned, fruits and vegetables cause problems since they contain water, which can cause spoilage or ice crystals when products are frozen—not to mention that these whole-food ingredients are expensive for food manufacturers. All businesses must be mindful of how operating costs affect the bottom line, and food companies may be under a greater burden than most, since American grocery shoppers and fast-food eaters have become deeply attached to the idea of inexpensive food.*

> Source: Melanie Warner. Pandora's Lunchbox: How Processed Food Took Over the American Meal. *New York: Scribner, 2013. Print. 6-7.*

Consider Your Audience

Consider this text carefully. Who is the audience? Choose a new audience for this information. It could be your classmates or siblings. Rewrite the information for your new audience. Change your tone, vocabulary, and sentence structure to make it fit your readers.

CHAPTER FIVE

PROCESSED FOODS AND YOUR LIFE

The aisles of most grocery stores are overflowing with processed foods. These packaged, easy-to-prepare items are convenient and delicious. But they can be unhealthy when eaten in large amounts. How can you incorporate processed foods into a healthy, balanced diet? The answer is moderation, or not eating too much of any one type of food.

Mixing whole foods and some processed foods into your diet is a smart choice.

Finding a balance between processed foods and whole foods is a healthy lifelong habit. Not all processed foods are unhealthy. Some are full of healthful nutrients. When eaten alongside whole fruits, vegetables, grains, protein, and dairy, processed foods can be a valuable part of a healthy diet.

Read the Labels

Paying attention to the foods you eat is an important step in balancing your diet. Nutrition labels are found on every packaged food product sold in the United States. They list the ingredients found in the product, as well as the calories and fats. Heavily processed foods often have long lists of ingredients. Some feature high amounts of fats and calories. Try to avoid or limit the number of heavily processed foods you eat. Instead choose minimally processed foods that are low in fats and calories.

Reading food labels is not always as simple as it seems. Some ingredients, such as fats, sugars,

It is okay to enjoy some processed or packaged foods every once in a while.

and salts, have different names. This can make them difficult to spot. To stay healthy, try to limit the amount of sugar you eat each day. There are many different names for sugar that can be found on a nutrition label: maltose, dextrose, evaporated cane juice, fructose, high-fructose corn syrup, brown sugar,

Learning to interpret nutrition labels can be very helpful in choosing healthy foods.

corn syrup solids, sucrose, raw sugar, molasses, maple syrup, and lactose.

Each meal or snack is an opportunity for a healthy choice. On days when you have a busy schedule, it might make more sense to eat processed foods. On other days, preparing a meal from fresh, whole foods is the better decision. Thinking critically about the foods you eat will help you stay healthy and make wise diet decisions.

YOUR LIFE
Interpret Labels

Step 1: Check the serving size. Compare it to how much you are going to eat. If the serving size is more or less than you plan to eat, adjust the rest of the numbers on the label so they are accurate.

Step 2: Look for the number of calories per serving. Low-calorie foods have around 40 calories. High-calorie foods have 400 or more calories per serving.

Step 3: Check the fats, cholesterol, and sodium. If a food has 50 percent of your daily value of fats, it is probably very unhealthy.

Step 4: The bottom part of the label shows the daily value of important nutrients.

- Processed foods are foods that have been altered to make them easier to consume. Heavily processed foods have been changed in many ways and often include a long list of ingredients. Minimally processed foods have been changed only slightly and often have few ingredients.
- Foods are processed to improve their flavor, texture, and aroma, to keep them from spoiling, to make them easier to prepare, and to add vitamins and minerals.
- Many processed foods contain high amounts of fats, sugar, and salt. These additives contribute to dangerous health problems, such as diabetes and obesity. Families who eat large amounts of processed foods typically do not cook very often. This means many children are not learning to cook healthy foods at home.
- Food scientists work to improve the taste, health, safety, and life span of food products. They often work for food companies, universities, and governments.

IN THE KITCHEN

Homemade Fruit Cocktail

1/2 cup strawberries

1/4 cup grapes

1/2 cup bananas

1/2 cup oranges

1/2 cup kiwi

2 tablespoons fresh lemon juice

1 tablespoon honey

Ask an adult to help you slice these fruits into bite-sized pieces. Then mix all the fruit in a large bowl. Drizzle lemon and honey onto the mixture and stir well. Cover the mixture and let it sit for 30 minutes in the refrigerator before eating.

STOP AND THINK

Say What?

Learning about the processed food industry involves many new and complicated vocabulary words. Look through this book and identify five words you have never seen before. Find each one in the dictionary and write down the definition in your own words.

Tell the Tale

Chapter Two of this book introduces key moments in the history of processed foods. Write a 200-word summary of how processed foods grew to become an essential part of many modern diets. Include details about important historical figures and popular food items. Write as many details as you can.

You Are There

This book discusses how early food scientists worked to create long-lasting and flavorful processed foods. Imagine you are a food scientist who is trying to create a new type of cookie. Write a journal entry about your work. Record your hopes and frustrations.

Surprise Me

Chapter Four of this book discusses the pros and cons of eating processed foods. Identify two pros and two cons that you found surprising. Write a few sentences about each fact. Explain why you were surprised and what you learned.

GLOSSARY

additive
a substance added to foods to improve their flavor, increase their nutrients, or keep them fresh

cure
to preserve

decaying
slowly breaking down

dehydration
the process of removing water

fermentation
a chemical change in foods using bacteria or other organisms

food science
the study of the makeup of food

fortified
having vitamins or minerals added in that are not naturally found in a food

lactose
a kind of sugar found in milk

nutrients
things that nourish, especially in food

preservatives
substances used to keep foods from spoiling

LEARN MORE

Books

Gold, Rozanne. *Eat Fresh Food: Awesome Recipes for Teen Chefs.* New York: Bloomsbury Children's Books, 2009.

Pollan, Michael. *The Omnivore's Dilemma for Kids.* New York: Penguin Group, 2009.

Shanley, Ellen. *Fueling the Teen Machine.* Boulder, CO: Bull Publishing, 2011.

Websites

To learn more about Food Matters, visit **booklinks.abdopublishing.com**. These links are routinely monitored and updated to provide the most current information available.

Visit **mycorelibrary.com** for free additional tools for teachers and students.

INDEX

ABOUT THE AUTHOR

Rebecca Rissman is an award-winning children's author and editor. She has written more than 200 books about history, culture, science, and art. She lives in Portland, Oregon, with her husband and daughter.